whether hatchling
or fledgling,
may something
in this work
be of value for you

A HAND MADE LIFE

learning to live unmediated

by Mealla Sweet

Published in 2023 by
Machete by Moonlight
the Bend of the Upper Deschutes, USA

Copyright © 2023 by Mealla Sweet

Cover image © Mealla Sweet

ISBN 979-8-218-18945-7 (paperback)

CONTENTS

INTRODUCTION

This is a work between works. As in so much of
that resonates with me, betweens are rather import-
nt of things. Thus, this is a trail I must clear my way
rough. A valley, a field, a riparian plain, as though of
ettles, in front of me. 'Tis a medicine I know and trust
ell though. So through it, I freely go. A trail I must
so leave as markings behind me. If for nothing else,
ut for my own self to witness the changing in move-
ent and the needful nature of that, if ever I move to
uiet my own intuitive listening again, or think about
ackstepping.

Like a diary of sorts. A smudging too. A clear-
ng of the air and mists in one gesture. Documenting
ntergenerational healing in real time, and a sampling
f the forces which are opposed to it. Without any need
or external conditions changed. Such an important
omponent of it. The meticulous steps it led me to
nake. The formality of purging poisons meant to bury
ove alive. But love survived. Love within me. Not
ontrolled by any. Wild and free.

If ever you find yourself at a similar crossroads
in that the content herein resonates somehow, or you
find yourself already having been caged in and sensing
it, may this sharing empower you to push on to find any
way best forward for you. Blessed are the resonance
fields that guide our own selfs distinctly through the
many trials we all endure as humans living in it.

WE CAN'T HELP BUT RISE

Not a soul alive
could've prepared me
for the relapses
like an endless sequence
of waves
one after another
with no visible
break in sight
that would ensue
after all that
threatening
to close mine heart
all over again

Death after death
like waterboard torturing
between life and death
death as though
angered
it could not kill me
on the one hand
yet on the other hand
as though
delivered also
by God's hand
this time
therefore

I'm left
only to wonder
was it always
like that

Divinity
a face of God
as though flesh like
apart from me
coming to me
dreamlike
playing all sides
myself included
who was on no side
smiling
ever graciously
loving me
knowing it all
necessary
showing me the strength
I lacked awareness
I had
within me
all along
and never didn't
because of where
it comes from

How easy it is
to be misled
I see so clearly
that
now
how strength too
like love at times
can be one's weakness

They can construct
roles
of near wickedness
all they want
but their tactics
to take and control
will be exposed
in the end

What is in motion
is beyond all
human control
and control even
of all the nations
combined
blocs for power
are but illusions
for leading hearts astray

IN CHOOSING MY SELF

There is an ever slight
uneasiness in me
unlike all previously
what is coming undone
what is wanting
to come through
make its way
out of me

'Tis felt
within the stillness
of the silence
in-being
in me
already
bubbling up
from its strength
in the root
through the trials
in the gut
did it hold up
it did
and
through the heart
and
through the chest

through the lungs too
then
it has been
from there where
it made its way
into the breath
pausing only
in the throat
as though asking
will I let it out
will I allow my self
to be vessel
for this

What choice
do I have in it

Don't let the mind
have hold of it
least of all
such important
of decisions
is it not we
who more often
than not
get in our own way

TRUSTING IN THE UNKNOWN
IN A WHOLE NEW WAY

I've found
life delivers us
more questions
than answers
we will ever receive
that sometimes
there's no authentic
experienced authority
for our questions
anyways
not even God
in some circumstances
maybe
sometimes
not even nature
my most beloved
of wisdom keepers

The very nature
of such questions
unanswerable
by the lot
steers us to quest
differently then

A fine line

illuminating
a need for
inner trusting
in the face
of any authority
externally
that is

TIME IS NEVER LOST

I wish I could convey
all the countless
hours
days
months
and more
spent
buying into doubt
to keep my own
light
down or out
sometimes
just to hold
my own self back
as though
subconsciously
choosing to further
listen
other times
at the demands
of
or
for
the seeming benefit
of others
different reasons
in differing seasons

But 'twas false
as that
and any requests
towards such amends
ever are
wasn't it

Though not time
wasted
either
as time can't
ever really be
not truly
not for anyone
being
brutally honest
internally

DOES DIVINITY MAKE OR BREAK CHAIN

I wonder at times
how some of the greats
teachers across lineages
Celtic at least
would respond
in our times
those in clear service
of Divinity
who defiantly
stood for oneness
carried forth that torch
when 'twas not
popular
in a merchant class
ordering of the world
would view it
now
that it is

How would they respond
to the chains
constricting in
like boas of sorts
as though round throats
though reigning more like
black mambas now
disguised

surprise attacks
aggressive
baiting
sneaker like
even when unprovoked
territorial
resolved to
take possession of
all thought that could be owned
by means of poisoning
or striking down at least
all that cannot
love not controlled
or willing to be taken
without consent
owned
as though that's how love
works at all
ever tempting
conformity
with darker than molasses
pulls
the deceptions
behind the sweetness
only visible
when one doesn't give in
to being owned

When the snakeheads
like snake oil salesmen
come on out
rear back at ya
not a moment before
never a moment before
so subtle
though
in times too
is it
so as to not be
visible
to others
being pulled in
fore it's never
just you
being worked that is

I had a dream
once
witnessing the moment
hindsight
black mamba medicine
moved in
to forever annihilate
that of rattlesnake
like Turtle Island

being imbricated
but the world really
a succumbing
black magick
overtaking
white magick
as the social normative

And I just saw an eagle
fly overhead
right there
in that very moment
for me having
confessed that
written it down
the dream
given to me
it's rare I share
such things
these days

Was this the interrelationality
the greats so dreamed
greats of all old
to cultivate
for soul wholeness
in the world

CONTROL IS ANTI-SOUL

Let the medicine
take hold of you
permeate into your depths
and watch
and witness
all the ways
the self resists
so guarded
have we become
to shy
away from it
and those that seek
to control it
well,
they're not helping
one bit
in our heart of hearts
centered
in who we most are
we know beyond
all means of knowing
control is against
God
is against
world soul
is against
all souls

WHISPERS ARE MANY

The land
speaks to me
sweet whisperings
as does the land
to so many
where none
can see
nor hear me
reminding me
the ways of courting
and who chooses
who
why choice
is everything

Oh, how humans
want to control
these things
so they can
control them
you
me
but the land
the land assures me
slow and steady
that the land too
the land too

has its own say
like Divinity
beyond
all
human controls
too does
in it

NO PAIN, NO REAL GAIN

We are never put through
more than we can endure
God hasn't the same plans
for any of us
so embrace the journey
that is yours alone

With each trial
the sacred within us
is forging us
into more
if humble enough
we are
to allow it

Worry not
of those
whom never fall
or rarely are pushed
to bleed
by others

We are not all carved
of the same clay
and therefore
our resiliencies
blessings

struggles
gifts
are neither the same
either

LEARNING GRACE

Some of us are
later bloomers
we don't all walk
the same roads
some of us ask
different questions
we've each
our own journeys
nor is father time
equitably
kind
to all of us

The sisters
as weavers
'twere more kind-hearted
but like when sitting up
all night
one learns
women
who once entrusted
it
to men
have been stripped
from
all most critical
of positions

in relevant councils
and we wonder why
ethics
have become so
unbalanced
but we're not doing ourselves
many favors
are we

It's okay
to bleed
and it's okay
to be devastated
through bleeding
it's okay to bleed
for asking questions
others would not
bleed
for asking

I'm of the perception
such contradictions
matter
like the color red
utilized
throughout nature
a warning indicator

like a lighthouse
as a beacon
or the northern star
moving differently
than others

Life can teach us
that there're blessings
in bleeding
while much
can be avoided
through silence
and reading
upfront obedience
there's something to be said
for experiential learning
little else
quite like it
not all paths
are as wise
as others
thus, having said that
I wouldn't recommend it

What of an untold art
though
hidden in shadows

of being good at
or having become
good at
bleeding
like Brigid's birthing
between thresholds
the tears
she must've shed
but how too
she must've been held

I am interested
these days
only
in things
that're worth their weight
in shouldering

MINTED

Awaken
blooming rose
the aptly
candlewax
that spilled over
onto that
black and white
tartan journal
on the day
I finally
stood up for my self
in body, spirit, and soul
as though blessing
a much larger
bodied
awakening
only time will tell
won't it

INHERING

Nature
comes second nature
to me
in that
I don't much
think about it
my place in it
its sheer beauty
and constantness
in my life
perhaps first nature
it's a bit more accurate

You'd think
I'd write
more about it
but 'tis not the medicine
I needed
such relations
infinitely
are
to me
unquestioningly
always there
with me

I feel in nature

wherever my feet
lead me
land me
it's where humans
have made it so
to feel not as such
those are the tensions
I'm interested in
loving a bit more

Why the fracture
between soul and nature
heaven and earth
either or
not together somehow
it's so distant
from how I experience
things
from how I see
inward
and
outwardly

DIVINITY'S PENDULUM

Stillness
movement
inward
outward
polarities
directions
little is as
it seems
but even greater a lie
is it
in my experiences
to suggest the need
'tis to erode
such differences
to make dualism
disappear
as though it could
as though it should
to make non-relevant

That is not elevating
nor consciousness
expanding
but the opposite
of freeing
to create smallness
in it

Freedom
true freedom
is movement
and stillness
possibilities
retained
along spectrums
and spaces between
the sacredness
in laws of attraction
and laws of opposites
need both measures
for energy to move
at all
for love even
to exist

DAMNED TRIBUTARIES

We are like salmon
ever returning
to a home stream
that gifted life
to us
knowing its scent
above all others
and while we may
adapt
if diverted
forcefully
ever will we be
be led
to remember
the spring
of our being
and the perfectness
of Divinity's orderings
of us
before imperfect
human hands
began forcing it

UNDAMN THE RIVERS

Control
'tis been
such an intuited
theme
sensed
to ever bring
presence
'round to
the consistent need
to do so
in so much
that comes through

Forces that restrict
movement
sensed so often
like the damming up
of tributaries
one after another
inhibiting
like water
our free flowing
nature
a river's ability
to forge its own course

Fore control

ultimately
externally inflicted
is anti-soul
is anti-matter
is anti-union
imposed
upon each
against Divinity
but so too
is control towards Divinity
mostly the same thing

All attempts
to seize love
moving in its own way
pretending any's love
is up for grab's
is up for taking
no agency
no choosing
no autonomy
'tis an ultimate abuse
especially through
thought terrain
controlling

Is that now why

the game was made
through all the pages
of recorded history
how it's now been
made
in our present day
made to be
anyways
for love to be
bullied
stolen
stealable
as though 'twas real
to control it at all
to agree to those terms
is Stockholm Syndrome
and not love set free
as Divinity
created life
to be

ESTRANGEMENT

Love shouldn't be
made to be
any gateway
for terrorism
against souls
taking at all
is that not
ultimately
against
world soul
when world soul
all but denies
world soul
what strange and peculiar
times
we live in

RADICAL SELF LOVE

Choosing Love
doesn't mean
the same thing
for much of any of us
as an American
as a European American
and let's be clear
about that
it's coming to mean
in the cultural tones
and the nuanced
pressurizing
build up to it
to choose others first
at all costs
to choose the healing
of others
over one's own
to choose seeing the divinity
in others
and not recovering it
within one's self
no,
that most of all
can never be allowed
all of these scaled out
too

to heritages
too
that's more how it
trickles down
who is
who isn't
allowed to

Its culmination
points towards
very much by those
who've taken control
over it
actively seeking
greater control
over it
to abandon
internal guidance
intuitions
our very own compasses
instead of wisening them
heartening them
growing them at all
interiorly within
it is to
without protest
or exception

without any room
for nourishing
self-worth
embrace
projections
and homogenizations
no matter our lived
or directly inherited
experiences
from others too
without all the answers
themselves
because nobody
has them
all worked out
without any reflection
either
or questioning allowed
conversely
and in doing so
it's to blindly empower
in others
all that has been
still is being
hunted in us

And we can know

'tis to these extremes
herein
still
not past tense
because subtlety guarding
against complexities
not feedback looping
in those ways
is anything but
tolerated
quite unlovingly so
it is thought terrain
controlling
terrorism against souls
amplified
demanded
'tis semantic ownership
to enslaved side-taking
demands transgressions
be always tolerated
or one's own self
is cast aside
as always the problem
the one being
unloving

It is the weaponization

of love and empathy
grounded in something
that is anything but
and it's a demand
that all that building up
to this
also be swept
under the unseen rug
without change in conditions
in time
in ways that are in
full agency
of the sum
of those doing so
so, I am sorry
but also,
very much not
to the fragile egos
when I set a boundary
that 'tis not love to me
and never will be
and it simply doesn't matter
not anymore

CHOOSE YOU FIRST

Do not choose
even love
before your self
fore love most of all
love even for Divinity
God if one must call it
begins within thee
each
therefore
to choose love first
outside one's self
'tis anything
but love
if God loves freedom
wouldn't God value
then
each choosing
love unmediated

Why all this
pretending
it to be
otherwise then
demanding more so
near mocking those
who don't comply
explicitly

The more covert
the abuse of souls
the more dangerous
chaining
it is
isn't it

MERRIMENT

There are a great
many challenges
in ever traversing
our richest
entanglements
best exposed
by laughably
examining
contradictions
in how boundaries
like borders
can be both
weaponized
momentum for controlling
their assertion
most effective for dividing
not global communities
but regional peoples
or once closely related peoples
or conversely
in their aims for dismantling
as though healthy boundaries
that there aren't such things
that there shouldn't be
not on any scaling
how love can be
armed

as transgression
instead of
a grander calling
to be so attuned
to have to
dig in
within
know thy self
know soul
know matter
and be empowered
to hold in suspension
that it all matters

I move forward
in merriment
a personal gaiety
released
are all the tears
it took
to get here

Beauty and wildness
have as many tones
as the finest
discerning
palette does

OUTSMARTED

That
Divinity frequencies
would labor
seemingly
as movement in it
to teach us
to keep us from
all that 'tis not
good for us
distinctly
it's near a miracle
at times
even through moments
it does not feel
as though
life is moving
too for us
in a good way

But faith
faith strengthens us
across our lives
to step into trusting
all is as
it should be
and through faith alone
our lives are opened

to unfold
leading each
where to it is
they best belong
laws of attraction
repelling and attracting
like atoms on the web

Any can try to control
any
all they want
but behind the scenes
behind the scene
all is perfect
in its unfolding

ANTIPARASITIC DETOX

We must all grapple with
the ways in which
cosmic
unfolding's
have rolled over
and cut at us
demons
that none are without
how we do or do not
entertain
their dancing too
with others
but already
I've said too much
haven't I

DELOUSING

Snakes and dastards
come after many
wanting to bury 'em
with enough tenacity
it's as though
subconsciously
'tis really themselves
wanting
needing
to be buried
just unable to see
themselves
as they are
in the present
or if they do
and have grown
tired of it
unwilling to be
honest
with others
about it

FLIGHT LESSONS

No different
could it've been
under no honest terms
would they've allowed
light in
in its wildness
uncontrolled
uncontrollable
by them
that was the sin
they tried to pin
is that now why
the hiding of lights
began
some could contend so
as I am
how unrelated giants
all became homogenized
to mean the same things
through literalism

But 'twas they
themselves
reframing it otherwise
whom
lacked faith
lacked openness

lacked eyes to see
beyond
what they already had
previously
having determined
it all figured out
at first sight
first test
first confirmation
as though first
feeling of power
surging within
clung to
through countless ages

Trust least of all
those who praise
never falling
fore all the lights
bright
known to the world
across time
were endlessly
tortured
persecuted
oppressed
and doubted

dying every day
sometimes
simply to rise again

Never falling
or being ripped to shreds
especially
in times like these
is no deedful sign
of having much of anything
truly worked out
more than any other
more so just illusions
for better taking
from others

THE TIDAL WAVES

They came
to shake my faith
they came to bury me
like they do so many
had I been them
surely
I'd of done
the same thing
but in that
I'm not them
nor are they me
maybe I wouldn't have
only they
will have to wonder
about that now

How painful it must be
for some
the personalization
experiences
of being
one tiny little part
of world soul
no wonder control
to contain it
that which it tolerates
became so

increasingly
the more power
they were granted
in it
instead of
its opposite
as was assured
would be the case

Those who tarnish
by controlling
owning love
trying to
mirror
those who tainted
by controlling
trying to
religion
the same
they've
they had
no right
to do so

Are there not as many
tears now
from the forcing

as a power bloc
for love
allegedly
as there too have been
and are
from priests
the world over
in and from all religions
were the raping's
really that different
who gave any
the authority
to abuse children
and adults alike
entire societies
like that

Of all the offenses
anti-God like
what if controlling love
is transgression
most of all
against God
against Divinity
surely against nature
God and All

UNCHAINING

The way
is to walk away
from all of 'em
to not let any play
a power play
as you not choosing
freedom in yourself
for yourself
not even many helpers
are without
similar agendas
in it
she most of all
taught me this

Trust less
those
who stage themselves
to take a higher road
while taking from you still
which means
others too
many many others
surely
all the while
playing as though
that's not

what they do   53

Let 'em have it
let 'em have all of it
leave 'em to all that they wanted
find solace in soul
and ever moving
towards
beauty
walk away from everything
if you must
into your most beloved
wilderness
naked
but clothed in faith
fore in your walking away
they have you not
but you do
you have you
and in doing so
you gain your freedom
in every way
that matters
unchained

THE NAMELESS

They hunt your imperfections
weaponize 'em
against you
as though they alone
need no reflection
as though they alone are
without 'em
that everyone
must choose
them
and all they say
that must be chosen
as all loving
over everyone else
over any other loving
or pay the deepest price
will one be coerced
to pay
by any means
deemed necessary

Such positioning
'tis a claiming
over you then
is what leads you
to feel
less than

to make you doubt
your self
in as many ways
as possible
by only
your mind's own haunts
if they can

When you grow
they hold it against you
that you grew at all
that you didn't rise
to their alleged opening
that 'twas never an opening
anyways
and ungrowing
do they then say
you are anyways
knowing how dehumanizing
subtleties can be
the workings
of their masterpieces
dehumanizing
by a thousand unseen cuts
instead of in honesty
why it hurts
and hurts so much

and is light years harder
to see
as the abuse that it is
by the self and the many
over abuse more obvious
a trapping for those
that also want to see
and believe
innately
in the goodness
of most others

How it all plays
into
false exaltations
that your love
was ever for them
and only them
and not that which
you heartfully cared for
not even
once proven
through trials
letting any love freely
not them
is the highest crime
there is

to be committed
in their eyes
and therefore in it
and by their demands
from God
their controlling of God
that is

Paying them
any attention
at all
if it now makes more sense
is where the problem
dwells
the lesson
that must be learned
if anything
at all
is prioritized
to be learned
from it
for any empathic
mind or heart at least
that wants to love
and love freely
when what you love
is what you're hunted for

what you are forced
to burn for
outwardly
for simply loving
so spiteful are they
knowing
in the deepest recesses
of their sensing
it is not them
but without eyes
to see why
and so again
no reflection
only projection
back on you
ya can't ever win

So illusions are made
to portray
it ever is
was
you alone all along
and the many like you
the pentimentos in place
so very necessary
for smear campaigns
to be most effective

smear campaigns
so telling of everything
though aren't they
the truth in relationality
which surface mind you
every time
you choose you
or love or beauty
in your eyes
unwilling to bend
to theirs alone
your eyes as the eyes
the eyes of the beholder
not theirs
for they've their own
but they won't leave you
to yours
and every attempt
to stay balanced
in your own eyes
it is you then
who is scapegoated
as trying to control it
their eyes and others
and in that alone
is how
they tear you down

if they don't have more
to do so already
with swifter ease

The only opening
ever intended
created
was for you to believe
there's more worth
in them
that maybe
you need them
though they never you
to not be tormented
outwardly
and that may not be
untrue
given their controlling
positioning
and the depths
of conditioning
that maybe you alone
are the problem
or those more like you
so you cede more of you
or endure far more
for refusing to

The danger
in seeing Divinity
in everything
is many won't
reciprocate
any willingness
to see it in you
in kind
it's a perilous pinning

In that,
growing renders it
hard
harder and harder
to relate again
in old ways
without transparency
of all that's been
endured
so most grow alone
in silence
fore what little
other choice
is there

How many
are so much

less alone
than they know

Is this
how communities
and families
are torn to pieces
day by day
year by year
through centuries
and millennia's
potentially
that none of this
is any new thing
fore what if
all the pages of history
untold
in folk songs
poetry
paintings
monuments
architecture
and living memories
all of them
in their truer weavings
together
bring light to this

exiled in shadows
untolerated

That sure would send
giant hearts
into hiding
wouldn't it
cause and effects
of creation
what they made
with it
and while I know
beyond all knowing
that God is in
everything
and while I must then
concede
that God too is then
the anti-Christ
it doesn't mean
any have to worship
nor honor
the anti-Christ
as any high expression
of Divinity
or God
do they

When all is said and done
what is more anti-Christ
than contradictions
weaponized
far different
than in honest error
isn't it

EXISTENTIAL CONFIRMATIONS

You know I once had
a wild deer
die in my embrace
not because it got shot
or hit by a car
but what I could only
relate to
as a heart attack
and I was the one
who came upon it
already in distress
I held it
as it crossed over
I knew intuitively
exactly what to do
and had no fear
it calmed with my touch
and so much of its pain
transferred to me
released
I learned so much
that day
things I'll never
speak of
it showed me

Divinity

has always been with me
guiding me
God of the game
none are to speak of
is not God to me
love can never be
stolen
controlled
contained
boxed in
doesn't work that way

Divinity is wild
and love is its language
no games necessary
actually,
I'm pretty sure
Divinity does not approve
entirely
of the game making
at present
and hasn't
for a very long time
scriptures even
cue us into this
but the game too
exists

so there's that
to grapple with

Divinity
has always been there
for all of us
leading us
as Divinity wants us
led
like the medicine
nature and divinity and ancestors
in trilogy
as God beyond
seized thrones and councils
protecting me
long ago
from staying along
going down
every wrong road
for me
not because of any wrong
in me either
but because of my own
niche beauty
and we all
have our own
to come to see

LIGHTENING THE LOAD

Learn to see
that all of life
across history even
'tis a game
even though a game
it also
very much is not
each life
best lived
regardless
as though 'tis
the only one
we've got
though and then
seasons too
it must have

What mark then
of participation
does one leave upon it

When we can grow
to see
smiles behind smiles
that were always
to be found
understanding

there're rules
unjust ones too
absolute
intentionally
constructed
taking abounds
the burdens
that are and were
never yours
will drift away
dissolve purified
like particles as illusions
on the winds
carrying them away

Then we can see
so vividly
the truer nature
of participation

Such an opening
though heart wrenching
initially
initiated me
blessedly
to witness
what freedoms

others too
prioritized
from that which
they did not

THE FOOLS FOOLS

They've labored so hard
to take control
of fields for love
over fidelity of souls
all the while
running around
amok
looking overly organized
overly polished
overly loving
prying
into lives
of those they also
want to bury
especially those
they want to bury
though love them
they'd say was the aim
you're missing the point
if you don't get it, they say
asking
pleading
all the while
where
does the conversation
go next
what is the next story

Demanding
assuring
their boundaries
unmoving
not needing moved
or even examined
all the while
ignoring
boundaries they transgress
mocking
projecting
finding grace
by due strength
gained
from taking
courageously

Yes,
you read that right
consciously and intentionally
from the contents
of their own hearts
taking necessary
the worst kind of it
as they'd never own
up to it
fueling their positioning

in creative surges
and beatings
leading one to wonder
if they'd have it
without it
a taking so intimately
that takes hold too
of the curve of it
again and again
fore control begets control
instead of on any
even playing field
does it occur

This,
is this what they made
from their dreams
for justice
equality forced
by advantages and handicaps
necessitated
that does seem consistent
though
doesn't it

THE MYSTERIOUS WEB OF WYRD

Of all that was shattered
into grief's grievous terrain
'twas the landscape of synchronicity
forever changed

They'll never be willing
to grasp
how their love
is more like
despotism and tyranny
stalking and murderous
than anything loving
how the slightest self-love
for one's own self
if not subdued
under them
explicitly
sends them spiraling
into
greater masks
projections
for fear
in holding their own
up
of having to see
their love
is anything but

loving
for some
and simply can't be

Not when the takings
abound
abundantly
why take at all
why not've left it
to Source
why not leave it
to Divinity
and true connecting
it'd have happened
organically
if they'd of done so
as all of life does
life's innate code
is to thrive
it's more often than not
humans in the way
preventing life thriving
from simply happening
by trying to control things

'Tis as though
they perceived

perceive
their wants and needs
and ways of knowing
more important
overall
how to right all wrongs
better than all
above Divinity
above all that is sacred
didn't they
don't they
preemptively controlling
by way of striving
in weaving
themselves into
being over you
thus over others too

Synchronicity itself
a most sacred of things
something I have lived
and put the trust of faith
in living my life by
synchronicity
weaponized
in the ways it can be
by all that is unseen

and unspeakable
about it
until one learns
to better see

Raw necessity
led me
to have to remove
the awe
of flow between humans
to have to listen
most deeply
to synchronicity
in only its ways
that are not able
to be controlled
by human influences
human interjection alone
how much time I spent
rejecting then
all human forms of it
running from it
even where I shouldn't have
where I knew early on
I should not have
because of how those wells
were being poisoned

I grieffully had to
halve that element
of source based
wonder and enchantment
in having to open my eyes
to what they've made
of human connection
of human love
the aims to take control
over
the rivers of life
itself
how those rivers flow
all around
between
and through us
and never again
can one look out
at creative works
nor many's
participation in life
in the world
the same again
there's a pain in that
to lose trust
in the beauty of creativity
and movement

for swaths of humans

'Tis painful
to've let go
of that awe
in human connection
as one finally moves
into most deeply
loving humans too
the irony of timing
is not missed on me
to have to learn to be
most weary
and untrusting of it
knowing what they've done
and do with it
how intentionally
they'd do such a thing
how pervasive
the reach is

But that letting go
'tis not a total loss
fore synchronicity
exists still
outside of their
entire spheres

of influence
and it's never left
it never abandoned me
it speaks to those
always
with the willingness
and wherewith to listen
a gift of having
well honed that
before humanity's
turncoat revolutionaries
had seen in me
what I did not yet see
in my own self

Their stagings
of synchronicity
laughably
say more about
their takings
at the end of the day
to me
than they do
the contents
of their hearts
the contents
of their souls

so too do their words
and works
of loving then
come off sloppily so
now
once seen
it's easy to see
something missing
something critical
something I'd never
cheat them
go out of my way
to reflect back for them
mirrors that we all are
and all
for one another
as humans
'tis not mine to do so
anyways
to mirror them
much of anything
moving forward
who is to say
'twould not be
mine own projections
anyways
leave them to their ways

I've my own path
to forge and enjoy
struggle within
and make my life upon
abundance and love
everywhere I look now
knowing anything less
is not worth my attention
in this short life we live
love that speaks
my heart's own language
and would
without really trying to
loves that can't not be
what they are
just as I leave them too
to enjoy the fruits
of theirs

Their power does not
woo me
tempt me
leave me to feel
missing out
on anything of importance
for me
nor does it

entice my fancies
nor strike awe in me
when one comes to see
what I've seen
there is no longing
to be in that know
nor their circles
only an urgency
to move away from it
all
towards
where the sacredness
of true synchronicity
leads one distinctly

Divinity
outside
of the invisible hand's
controlling
the only place it has
real meaning for me
anymore
the deepest of lakes
the purist of them
so clean one can drink
right from them
still

without any filtering
without any boiling
the richest of wells
such waters are
and never before
have the tragedies of life
looked more beautiful to me

DISPELLING THE CYCLE

Even playing fields
I'm quite certain now
they fear most of all
those who uphold it
to favor takers
to put 'em at the front
of the great hand's movements
to shelter them
from all reflection

But never mind me
there I go again
giving into the weaknesses
of black magick's working
making
in the world
this work
this work is about
that transition for me

It's good to be tested
again and again
with it
removing toxins
from every fiber and cell
each drop of blood
each strand of sinew

from bone marrow
to the living memory
of water in us
removing those toxins
matters immensely
to make more and more room
for all
that is growing within
no longer
without
as it never was
anyways

There is always the beauty
to be seen
of those once snared in it
who don't participate
in life
the same
that they had the strength
to push on
once seeing it
even if distantly
is an unending inspiration
that any of us can
too

PERSPECTIVE

On more than one occasion
I have closed mine eyes
and soared
as though seeing through
the eyes of an eagle
wingspan immense
looking out
like an astronaut
looking upon
all he's ever known
so small
compared
to where
he's now flown

IMPENDING FEES

How I would love
to write love letters
unrequited or not
'twould not matter
to gift you
all the beauty
I witness in you
the ways in which
you are unlike others
even in the ways
you're scarred
especially in those ways
you can't see
what I see
without all that love then
being seized
being taken
as though any of us
were for the taking
like my ancestors
nabbed up
not even paid for
adult or child
so very long ago
a necessary mirror
to have seen
to have leaned into

fully
a not yet
resolved
holy debt

Love unchained
'tis not the world
I've known
this go 'round
more its opposite
love chaining
anything
to make it fit
into predetermined slots
like ballet boxes
to be owned and had

Into a war zone
I was born
'tis all my ancestors
near and far
have long known
for longer
than I care to know
and all I want to do
is love
freely

unchained
without new chains
being put on
for loving
at all
especially in ways
others are permitted to
without chains
put upon them
for doing so

THE ROUND TABLE SQUARED OFF

You see
one can't love
can't love their own
openly
well, not all can
true poison
in humanity
Divinity made
anti-Divine
the markings of
an anti-Christ
when they've set up
love
all love
any love
to be hunted or stolen

Love chaining
is all that 'tis
or sent forth
then are
attempts to bury
attempts to kill
all that won't conform
to such chemistry
all that won't embrace
their own enslavement

to love as stealable
and directionally restrained
how families
got torn apart
isn't it

Love
to be freely
expressed
as Divinity intended
before humanity's Adam
brought weakness to it
the table
that is
refusing to love
Creation
as Divinity
had asked
had ordered things
organic arrangement
and we wonder
why now
the world's such a mess
why so many
stay as far away
from choosing love
as they can

because love
love most of all
has been constructed
to be contained
how love has been made
to be against
all competencies
for how love
actually moves
in and between
us
souls
in human form
and souls
moving towards
Divinity unmediated

THIS BEAUTIFUL MAD WORLD

Everyone's
doing
their own thing
chasing their own
dreams
running from
their own hauntings
all the while
interacting
in an endless web
of entanglements

I undid myself
for the whims of inquiry
something felt off
I'd sensed it
for a good while
it's all my own fault
and I slipped into
a deepened sadness
all over again
unlike any
for a long time
because of what I saw

Far more are privy
than they let on

I laugh at projections
I witness others
putting on others now
quite often
or spraying about
at all
just as I laugh at many
conversation starters
and creative works now
how little of it matters
though matters to each
does it I guess
though maybe more
inside
do I laugh now
so as not to
give it away

Everyone's fucking crazy
everyone
like onlookers looking in
from without
foreign to such ecology
wouldn't know a food forest
from a destitute wilderness
not even most indigenous
these days

It's different now
that's how undone I came
gave up damn near everything
except what the universe
gifted me in it
my life's greatest blessing

INCOMING FAX

A marrying
of sky and earth
within me
within each 'tis possible
without mediator
as they insist
is them
even if it's preferred
to keep me exiled
or you perhaps
I've been shown
differently
the love within me
'tis beyond their reach
for taking
'tis out of taking's
reach

Its wholeness
more whole
becoming more so
with each passing day
I understand why
the burying
is wanted
of those like me
and it's nothing

of what they'd say
so much conspiring
to make it
that way
but I'm still here
heart still beating
lungs still breathing
with all the love
one could need

I've leaned into the arms
of loving
where projections
are seen
for what they are
and not
what any others
want them to be
truth is bound
in resiliency

We've till the end
each of us
and low blows
are but cheap shots
more reflective of those
who deliver them

GROW SMALL

All I can do now
is take one step
at a time
it doesn't scare me though
though I circle through
waves of anger
and more
as I make my way out
for it having happened
at all
but I'm also
grateful
and I really mean it

Never before
have I understood
silence more
terrorism against souls
forced to live
in contradictions
beside others not
turning each
against each
it's real
and it's long been
'tis nothing new
about it

Silence saves lives
more than anything
though silence sets
a different stage
for delusion making
future forward
their reasons
for having made it
that way
likely

Not even love
is strong enough
to survive
what silence can
regardless
silence survives
what love cannot
because love
as it's been staged
kills too
when love is weaponized
as a vote to be had
owned
against freedom
and love altogether
love can be a weakness

too
the greatest maybe
when terrorism against souls
is upheld
by the highest powers
the invisible hand
which are sometimes
grassroots too
portending otherwise

Never before
have I loved more wholly
I've full compassion
and empathy
for that which I love
and love most fully
don't really care
what those I love
have done
saints or sinners
unconditional love
exists
is born
within
for our own selfs
and 'tis grown
through enduring

terrible tyranny
together

Is that not where
silence
comes in
how some use silence
to isolate and abandon
to close thy heart
essentially
while others are willing
to offer and sit
beside us
through it
and yet silence matters
because of how some
invoke black magick
to feed off any
who breach silence
or would even dare think
about breaching silence

Let them be as right
as makes them feel
righteous
all of 'em
everyone at the same time

PROVIDENCE'S BLESSINGS

To be brought into
a light
to better understand
the invisible hands
behind life's workings
is to come to be able
to better appreciate
all that one has
lived through
and endured
no matter how terrible
experiences may seem

Abusive relationships
even
can be valued
as Divinity
helping us along
learning more about
substratums
seen and unseen
for better choosing
for one's own soul
where their higher self
is better served
to move towards
and steer clear of

Even the most
abusive hands
have Divinity's markings
behind them
for any being honest
within
the all is in all
and can't not be
nothing is not sacred
you see
Divinity
the best of it
sometimes
steering us
to see
what need be seen
to steer our own selfs
towards
and away from
depending on resonance
of what survives it

I sense in those
who labor to control
over others
an unwillingness
to make peace with that

WHERE INNOCENCE GOES TO DIE

Heaven wasn't made
to hurt like hell
was it
what if that's what
the unjust
made with it
not the heaven
for soothing
the inevitable hurting
of living
that it once
was entrusted
to be
the trails
of council corruption
so many sacred works
forewarned about

BROKEN DREAMS TOO ARE A BLESSING

Everyone's
in such a rush
these days
the world is ending
'tis ending
they say
and maybe it is
but maybe 'tis not
until it does
it hasn't
and I wouldn't
be so quick
personally
living to treat
matters
as though it is

Some say
they can't dream
until some
come home
but I'm more inclined
to perceive that
as untruth
of their own
test
in it

We've all been
delivered
broken dreams
but a truer question
'tis
what will each do
with that

Not to make light of it
yet
as in a honeymoon
state in love
'tis easy to love
before trials
put relations
to test
much more telling
is it
what becomes
in each
and in relation
between
when life
has broken
hearts to bit
what each make
from having lived that

THE LAND OF EXILES

I step out
beyond
into a wilderness
of my own soul's
making
choosing
my own way
machete in hand
as through a pathless land
as though it were
a choice
anyways
naked
but clothed in faith
blanketed
in warmth and grace

Fearing neither
sun nor moon
nor darkness too
though stars
less and less visible
are they
noise as light pollution
as the outer world
has come to making
night skies

less and less visible
haven't they
diminishing
circadian rhythms
as though all but
constructed light
is feared
these days

Source in everything
and therefore
Divinity's companionship
unending
laughter
beneath the veil
sensing
behind all scenes
watching it all
play out
perfectly

FLY HIGH

All the chatter about
birds chirping
songs galore
beautiful
in their own right
everyone of 'em
but not all songs
'twere made
for freeing
for soaring
where eagles fly

The air
'tis thinner up there
requiring
a different
strength of heart
to keep lungs
breathing
without
supportive oxygen

The balancing
that all mountaineers
must learn about
whether through
well prepared planning

listening
to those that've
been there
or the brutality
of humility
learned
experientially
both still learn
regardless
or freeze
up on those mountains
do they

DIVINITY'S SPECULUM

For all the humans
that've ever lived
perhaps 'twas Adam
who was weakest
of all
in heart
rejecting love first
its blossoming
its thriving
on its own terms
becoming blind
even if
eyes seemingly open
needing
love persecuted
reconstructed
oppressed
domesticated
love placed
under his thumb
to allow himself
to stand for love at all
the feminine fractured
from within still
then
as a result
with Lilith's exile

and made unduly
submissive
by Eve sinning
her empathy used
against her choosing
her own freedom
just to help him
feel love at all
so as not to be
killed
or exiled
or risk to look
unloving herself
even if she was unsensing
blinded by light in the light
of all that led up to her
being his

But then Lilith's love
and freedom too
were to be used
against her too
how another Medusa
was made
one told to be hated
and hateful
by near all

so that Adam alone
could exalt himself
above all others
and not look upon
all that came before
and after him
upon
his own reflection
in the most sacred
wellspring
of all

THE MUCH NEEDED HOLOGRAM

The sacredness
in darkness

Have you ever considered
the possibility
that to be forced
into exilement
was a most blessed
gift
in that
Creation itself
would be able to witness
the long arc view
of what those
on all sides
would do
with their positionings
not in one moment
but in the many
patterned
and not simply one
but all that each
is a part of
scaling all the way
to the whole
what is chosen
to be seen

or not seen
as to the contents
of the processes
for making it
the mess
that it will've
become

What if living
in exile
is a gift
an inkling
for the deepest of trusting
in those sent
into exile
that those exiled
into darkness
were not to look
to those that'd come
before them
but into their own selfs
above all else

Each understands not
what is not for them

A PROCESSION

Leave it up to Euros
to transmutate
exilement
into
peregrination
time and time
again
what if exile
was no punishment
more like a
sustained examination
imperfect steps
terrible ones too
necessary
as would it be
for many
and obviously
for any made blind
intentionally
and left on their own
in a cold cold
world
is it the why behind
our children were stolen
but also, a necessity
if any proving ground
'twas it

MY CHRIST IS THE LIGHT OF MY LIFE

What if it was Adam
himself
who turned his back
on Divinity
on humanity
on wildness
on loving freely
humanity's beloved
Adam himself
who could not love
wholly
as Divinity
had tested him
before him
could not allow love
to be free
to be most
itself

What if humanity's
Adam
was Balor
in human form
trying to make all
all in his image
instead of letting
Divinity and love

flow freely
unmediated
and uncontrolled
instead of inverting
free love
magickly
to be exiled as hatred
as hatred for some
but notice still
not hatred for all
never has been
but its opposite
for some
far too long has it

What if humanity's
Adam
was the world's
first serpent
in human form
have you ever considered
that possibility
that it was the fruits
of his garden
Eve herself
had to be made
of his own rib

after all
for him to embrace her
far different
than a kin analogy

The old timers
say it was said
that in Adam
all would die
but that in Christ
all would be made alive

SEEING ALL IN ALL

If we are serious
about healing strife
between nations
religions
human to human
relations
we must be so brave
in courage of hearts
to break cycles
in invocations
black magick making

By way of Adam
was Eve blamed
where then
by way of Eve
was the serpent blamed
but the serpent
was of the fruits
of Adam's garden
made for his making
of his own bed
after having rejected
already
Divinity's love
as 'twas presented
before him

so it all got blamed
on the Devil next
as though
outside of him
instead of integrating
shadow awareness
that all of 'em had it

Is that the why
behind
all as competition
is that the why
behind
the breaking
of all nations
is that the why
behind
why 'tis a game
at all

In the game
as it is
be ever weary
of those standoffish
or postured in loving
that not all
love openly enough

to their liking
in the manner
where love's been made
to be caging
for cage them in
is that spell casting
still intending
on behalf
not of
freeing love
freeing movement
dynamism
but of ever
enslaving it
under the thumb
of those hellbent
on containing it
for their control
over all
'tis simply not loving
at all
not in my experiences
how all that has
ever been
on this earth
has been reduced
to this

BALOR'S OVERCOMING

'Tis not our job
to change
not even evil
'tis not our job
to shoulder the need
to even confront it
not anymore
for evil is also
in him
of course it is
as 'twas in Adam
the all
in everything

Some say
what we see
is what we become
is what we then are
but to see
Divinity
beyond all veils
beyond all heavens
beyond where
any phoenix flies
is to see it
in everything
and one can't not

be that
ever

Beautiful and terrible
just like nature
too is
as are we each
yet we can see all that
and still not
become it though
the worst in it
maybe we must
see it
to do so

A truer question
then
is
can one truly
rise above that
trial
not becoming terrible
that is
without integrating
their own terribleness
within
foundationally

How differently
the light
would find us then
seeing we are
but guests through darkness
exilement even
meant to show us
that to learn
how to not need
to give into
or give credence to
black magick's
workings
on us
against us
and most of all
through us

But what of those
in alleged full light
who work with it
as though 'twere light
itself
upholding its workings
constructed light making
to tear others down
to keep some small

and bury more
as the way
for others to grow
but not just to grow
either
to take hold
over others
and love
itself
a whole different level

Well,
everything is paid for
eventually
isn't it
at least that's what
some
say
though personally
I'm not holding
my breath
not any chance on that
not after
what I've seen
I don't think
I believe that true
at all

128   Unchaining love
       is all that matters
       to me
       and my faith
       in it
       that it matters
       foundationally

GREAT BASIN KENNING

Into no man's land
I went again
a place
I'm no stranger to
a place
I live at present
so close to the edge of
anyways
a land where
no waters
make their way
melodiously
to any sea
not a sea teaming
with life that is
quite a different energy
to it
but it was there
amongst all this
Wild West
expansiveness
I felt solace
and disarmament
from out of the weariness
of being projected
into an exilement
for refusing to agree

with their transgressions
in it

Let them be
as right as they want
to be
fore it's their own need
fore what does it reveal
but their own unwillingness
to allow another's sovereignty
disagreement weaponized

The smile
one can make room for
then
inwardly
becomes a priceless refuge
as do those too
who share in it
love being so dishonest
makes but more space
like clearing out a room
or clearing out the air
a smudging of sorts
the sweetest release
for one's own love
to grow more fully

if one allows
all things
in all ways
to be
sacred teachings
there's no worry
for those
who do not

And 'tis when and where
I finally saw it
I saw my skin aglow
the color of indigo

SOUL MIGRATION

It's been said
that darkness
is
where migration
of soul
occurs
then
if 'tis so
would we not
rather
look to the dark
as opposed to the light

Like grasses
pastures
in late august
who are in good need
of rest
after a long stint
of growth
and drought
some would outright die
so stagnant
and malnourishing
does growth potential
become
without winter's retreat

to just keep pushing on
through an eternal
scorching
summer sun
it's not lasting

As within
any single life
there must be
seasons
circadian rhythms
or the soul's
glow
loses it
particularity
and all
is made
poorer
for it

KNOCKED DOWN, NOT FALLEN

I don't actually think
I believe the world
to be fallen
not in the senses
of as we've been
told
each soul
perhaps
unwell
is the world
but not fallen
into wrongness
more so lowered
by loving hands
so gently
but then violently
shaken
by those who took
charge
to control
as the invisible hand
a test
Creation yet
has to humble them
with
has to humble many
with

What if the state
of fallen soul
has not to do
with soul distinction
joy or passions
but rather
the omittance of freedom
freedom of movement
in loving
dynamism empowered
so not exactly movement
either
movement of a different nature
more so
than superficial taking from it
omittance then
an aim to inhibit
world soul
itself
from its own migration
but also then failing
isn't it
the flowing of source
an inevitability
not even living in exile
can wholly deny
to any

NODAL SUPERCHARGE

When you finally learn
what your biggest
triggers are
and why
embrace it
explore it
lean into it
and tell no one
this is no era
for being
so vulnerable in
as all medicines
have taught me

Our triggers
aren't
for the world
to know
nor cater to
fore within those layers
somewhere
are your unique
superpowers
if one can be
so self-honest
to get into the roots
of 'em

their essence
in essence
the womb
the cavern explored
for unlocking
presence
of your gifts

It only took
the greater part
of a decade
to not look out
for those of others
but to look in
for mine
with clarity
like the piercing acuity
of an eagle's vision
so be patient
with yourself

When you see your own
there should be a calmness
about it
fore such medicine
of seeing in such ways
empowers

limitlessly

Freedom indeed
is costly
no matter the skills
about them
no one else
can see
the world
through your eyes
distinctly
nor should one
want them to
when precision
of your own
is awakened
authentically
within you

DECANTERING

To stand in
and be
an inconvenient participant
few know much
what to do with it
just as few
know how to do so
without great trials
of wandered solitude

Once you're shown
way to grace
to be sheltered
within it
through projections
and downpours
that through all of it
Divinity
will hold you
someway
somehow
one can learn
to fully allow then
any
their choosing
of relationality
with even one's self

without attachment
for their choosing's

To sense
across all senses
the world has been made
to be curbed
conformity essential
in our times
most of all
far more than prior
and increasing
as momentum
for side taking
for even love
is increasingly caging
but for an empath
any empath
being honest within
conformity is chaining
is downright painful
for whom freedom matters
immensely
built into the code
of deepening empathy
like boundaries too
how much they matter

to allow
to witness
to be
to see
the divinity
in each

Control is against
God and the all
in all
its myriad of ways
how many choose
black magick
as their energy source
in it
or get trapped
in it
before any choice
was it
to grow powers
for restraining
grassroots too
those most effective
need not be
one's burden
or way
once mapping is felt

for how it moves
but 'tis not until
one sees it
its twistedness
that they alone
can free themselves
from it
and its workings
on them
a bleeding from witnessing
I would wish upon
no other
all that cannot
be unseen
once seen

THE MEDICINE OF ALL MEDICINES

There is an infinite
unending medicine
for terrorism against souls
a God so freeing
so wild
so as to be
beyond
contradictions
Divinity
beyond human
counciled
controls
where any mediation
between
imposed
will reveal itself
ultimately
as the untruth
it is
or will've become
the road to hell
was paved
with good intentions
allegedly

Divinity beyond God above God
perhaps

being as though
God above God
appears to be
pulling strings
for controlling
flowing
Source itself
beyond any naming
any containing
any mediation
any governance scheduling
loves absolute
wildness
in my experience
not wildness
because it says so
'tis wild at all
but wildness
proven
through one's heart

How they got it
wrong
in honest error
perhaps
but held up dishonestly
regardless

to be eventually
revealed
as all things are
in due time
at least that's a prayer
I've put out there

DISCERNMENT IS SACRED

The moment
another
tries to define
the workings and details
of God's hand
in or over
the life of
another
over being
such an important
indicator
a tuning into
personal aims
for positioning
their human embodied
making
is a moment
they become lost
differently
and happen it does
every day

Being misunderstood
'tis such a blessing
when one is shown
to be understood
or guided

by all that matters
truly
how world soul
and Creation
outside of them
interacts with them
directly
distinctly
removed from
all projections
imposed and interjected
from others
being as though each
is as imperfect
as their own self
is

To say so
is not to do the same
fore 'tis to strip
outside authority
from being
unjust mediators
between
for one's own soul

The lies of those

that would labor
so intentionally
to riddle any with doubts
of where even
their trust or love
should or should not
reside or land
'tis a journey
none
can undertake
for another
in deciphering

FOREVER YOURS

Now that I know
just how intricately
it's all up to me
I'm slowing
my own
self down
no need to rush
even if
I've an honest
inkling
not to be spoken
of
of where it is
I may be going
like the pollinator
that needs night skies
to orient
to witness fully
bioluminescence
whose body
and sensorial experiencing
innately
knows the difference
between constructed light
and Divinity's offerings
illuminations
that sustaineth

all of Life

All that is
meant for us
will be there
for us
when we are ready

Someday
I will stand before you
fully and holy so
my anam cara
of all life
and no care
will there be
for how long it took
or why

The smile
waiting for you
'tis already inside
felt intimately
and growing
like the infinite
blossoming
it is

OUR GENERATION
OF WOUNDED HEALERS

I am a healer
by nature
didn't really choose
the path chose me
I guess that's what happens
when one must walk it
out of bare necessity

Someone once told me
I was a bit different
than many he met
on his path
years older was he
than me
a healer of healers
he referred to it as
though I would not
necessarily agree

A healer himself
regardless
went on to help
many
as he too had helped me
in his dying request
long had it been

since we'd last
seen one another
surrounded
by a community
of healers
was he
he pulled me in close
for one last ask
whispered in me ear
upon word of his
leaving this life
imminent then
on that hospital bed
that I'd head out
into the desert
and bless
his crossing over
that no one else but me
did he trust this prayer to
did he know
would know what to do
without trying to

I have midwifed
life
and
death

with awe and humility
intimately close
and from distances
in all I have seen
and life
life has been
beautiful
to me
even in
its worse moments

IT'S SO SIMPLE IT'S HARD

'Tis so easy
to get lost
in heritage
and loyalty
as is its opposite
the abandonment
of all of it
for the very same reasons
it's why understanding
love
unmediated
through one's own self
matters so much

It alone
if ruthlessly
honest
enough
can overcome
those dogmas

Dogmas whom
both
rear their heads
in near equal proportions
with all too frightening
similar outcomes

though isn't it peculiar
we've only been
forewarned
to see the former
and never the latter
like half of heart language
kept at bay
locking hearts away
from their better selfs
and the keys thrown away
so conditioned are we
contrasted in understanding
free flowing natures
like wild rivers
and source itself

Living in exile
as a daughter
in shadows
taught me this
and more
so too did projections
demanding loyalty
to being controlled
loyalty to control
and nothing more
no notion of heritage

allowed at all
one directionally
as well as the feedback
from having walked away
knowing each's soul
'tis not for sale
but also critiques
objecting the themes
that some shouldn't
love as they do
because loyalty
allegedly
appeared not present
as in utterly lacking
like half of heart language
kept away

They say
it's been said
that to believe
in
integrity
in heritages
is a grave sin
that will leave all
who do
or those locked out of it

from doing so
abandoned
falling into
their own demise
but is it that terrible
to be looked over
by the invisible hand
when the hand as such
is controlled
as so
that we now know
it is

What of being held
then
by Divinity itself
there are gifts abounding
out of reach
of any's controlling
defining
containing
in that
that are worth more
than all constructed
measures of gold

So much talk of love

it's damn near
everywhere
as are the rulings
of all deemed
not loving
which really amounts to
all that is tolerated
being the determiner
anything not agreeing
to be boxed in then
'tis not so tolerated
dead roots are they
not awakened they say
with next to no depth
allowed
in it

Is love not one
of the more nuanced
complexities
of existence
flowing
how then
does that
make any sense
to define it so
limitingly

SUBSTANCE

I am most interested
in things
worth their weight
bleeding worth
bleeding for
tearing worth
tears shed for
heartening worth
so too
heartening towards

That is where
you will find
this wild hearted
spirit

All woman
and
surrendering
along a topography
unseen
growing
in my love

DISENCUMBERING WILDNESS

There is so much
to revive
about wildness
wild nature
the wild in us
what it is to be
wild in spirit
in our loving
in how we relate
between things
to be wildly in love
with Divinity
and how Divinity
responds to all that
in varying degrees
and spectrums

I have been
hovered 'round
by wolves
like hyenas too
wild dog packs
like feral house cats
plagued with toxoplasmosis
submerged
in indigenous heart strings
teachings and pullings

of allowable varieties
into comparative mythologies
Sophianic mysteries
and a myriad of takes
on the wild feminine
at that
amidst
all the many blessings
of the Wild Wild West
fully engulfing me
and still
nothing measured
in wildness
to the nature and love
that Divinity
brought to me
loved in kind
back in me
sat by my side
as was worked out
all the illusions
held
as to how
all previously mentioned
fell short
in the ways of wildness
in loving

and therein taught me
the grace
to love
not fear
the wild heart
in me
unleashing it

It was
He alone
who wanted anything but
to tame me
contain me
and in those lessons
I grew to see
through my own
window and way
through so many perversions
of religious teachings
and the pages of history
about them
into our present day
now pervasive throughout
and in that
reflection
I found
unbound

compassion
within
for all the rejection
projections
and takings
I've endured
so many endure
a reality
He too
knows intimately

CONSCIOUSNESS SHORTCOMINGS

His glory
or Nature's
clung to
too tightly
that some eyes
are so open
they can no longer see
delusion or blunder
from within
or around them

There is a silver lining
is there not
to be witnessed
through all hardships
through all trials
dare I near say
Providence
my younger self shuddering
no matter the difficulty
in circumstance

Darkness is essential
and my own small self
can only ask
if 'twas a part
of Divinity

blessing humanity
like a coyote does

There is a part
of me
that'll always
cherish darkness
that darkness alone
makes way for light
to come in
like the moon and stars
and northern lights
by darkness do they
come to dance
to be seen
to do so
anyways
there is life giving
need
for diurnal rest
that any in touch
with their own
circadian rhythm
come to witness
ultimately
and the denial
of it

its glorious
sacredness
like exilement
can lead to its own
blindness
wherein eyes open
in broad daylight
of an unending day
slowly will take
away
all gifts of life
of Being
in it
'tis akin to cling
too strongly
like modern cities
now do
or stories to fear
such things
too did

THE CAKE I SENT BACK

The only pi
I'm interested in
is that of an
infinitely
unending nature

WATERSHED MOMENT

Let the rivers flow
feel the movement
of it all
as it arises in you
moving through you
filtered through
your chemistry
like a crystal
reflecting light
when we allow it to
be still with it
and fast
if need be
no need to control
its frequencies
Divinity is not
stagnant
Divinity is not
static
least of all
in the ways
it moves through
everything

Divinity moves
like water
moves between

all states
water is life
after all
mostly made of it
Divinity speaks
all languages
none own the language
of Divinity
nor Divinity's name
nor Earth
nor thought terrain

What if
all aims
to control such things
are anti-Divinity
in all ways

WINGS OF GRACE

When grace finds you
carries you
like eagle's wings
gifted
lifting
gifting strength in it
little more is there
to disrupt you
once embraced in it
once one allows
their self
to embrace it
that is
because
'twas always there
was it not
fore none can take
only ever can any
pretend to
temporarily

Illusions abound
but even stronger
is resiliency
a grace to dance
as any participant
can in it

and to simply be
free
choosing one's self
and one's own way
including in loving
especially in loving
before choosing
anything else
before choosing even love
blanketingly
outwardly

'Tis the ultimate
action of loving
of loving most fully
wherein any occurrences
externally
out of one's own control
which is near everything
then comes to matter
little

Freedom
to not choose it
was Eve's truer sin
the original
and only lasting

sin in it
in my very small
human
and womanly
opinion
in it
the easiest also then
to reclaim
and therefore reclaim
innocence
and virginity
the deeper meaning
within it

YOU WERE ALWAYS ENOUGH

When we understand
that all of Divinity
is within each
'tis no surprise
that the nature
of any
too
can be drawn up
from the wells
within

He walked amongst
men
in ways so relatable
but also
not at all
they either loved
or hated
Him
projections abounded
Divine masculine
in Medusa form
like many have known
put upon them
Krishna, Shiva, Vishnu
all in one
Brahma like

blasphemous right
like the many faces of Shakti
one amongst the many
partakers in divine ordering
all and none

Every time
He
breathed
colossal leaps
for unchaining love
each romantic movement
crumbs across time
wild trails to find
so quick were authorities
from all directions
to put a squash on it
sending societies
back into Dark Ages
just to do so
so threatening
was it
apparently
in that such extremes
were deemed necessary
like the most loved
and hated

of avatars

Christ energy
more liberating
and union inspiring
and freeing therefore
as all union in love
can't help but be
in honesty
than what any
controlled offerings
could ever offer

Nothing one can do
'tis ever enough
if freedom
in love and life
matters at all
they will only ever
try to come for you
kill your joy
undermine healing
you've already done
harm you
anyway they can
including
gang like bullying

leading into
then abandoning you
for not conforming
to their terms and demands
for how you must love
like Adam once did
proving the conditional
caging
love it 'twas
all the while
portraying
'tis your sins
you must pay for
and if they can't
succeed
tearing you down
by your own mind
falling into agreement
through all that
notice that falling
in line
is where falling
comes into play
they'll harm you still
through smear campaigns

What were the

witch and werewolf
trials
really about
or giants
for that matter
were they all the same
are humans so easy
to label and contain

There's something
darker
than can be imagined
in all this black magick
of which they'll deny
they work with
at all
they've become so blind
eyes open
they don't even remember
what it is
so long ago
'twas set in motion

Your very healing
of awakening to it
becomes an obstacle
in that force fields

of it cast
all around
and upon you
if one dare show signs
of overcoming
resiliency
they double down
to inflict it
again

Such hate
so subtle
so few can see
given how busy
lives are made to be
and
given the masks
and thrones
over love,
not in it,
of it,
they have seized

THE BUTTERFLY EFFECT

What is it to be
diaspora
something we shapeshift
in and out of
at our convenience
something others
tell us
what we are or aren't
and it is
something those not exiled
alone define
something of an
entitlement
without any responsibility
nothing at all

And what of the terribleness
of blood quantum
does it matter
in claiming or denying it
is it truly
only so deep
does no blood matter
either
do such things matter
not at all
has not the determination

to erase heritages
been as violent
and hateful
and ignorant
as the textbook cases
a worldwide list of 'em
for clinging to them
has been framed
to've been
taking the carefulness
of tending
out of it
and relegating
most of it
as toxic
so as to force
any care
into emotionally charged
reactive caging's
or intellectual numbness
for those denied it
or simply silence

How different love
for such things
could be
and between each

if such love
wasn't a primary
source
for being hunted
for some
for many
moving towards
world soul
and if it is hunted
in some
shouldn't it be
hunted in all
in equal proportions
or vice versa
not at all
why ever isn't there
heartening and wisening
around these such
most sensitive of matters

YOU ARE ANOTHER ME

Only a wild heart
can reach
a wild heart
you see it
when you know it
within
not simply wild
of nature
because one declares
'tis so
but of a different
nature
wild in the heart
wildly in between
things
which many want
to be
semantically
but so few
actually
move as such
holistically

A GALE WIND

Belonging is a choice
to belong
or not belong
not belonging
a rather obvious
arrangement
outcome
but belonging
belonging requires
tending
tending that which one
resonates
to belong with
with important
fore 'tis towards
in movement with
as in dance
sovereign in body
reciprocally consensual
complimentary
if one can
then 'tis not a to
is it
belonging to
one way
linearly
we're learning
aren't we

BEING FASTIDIOUS

I am like
that space in between
like the ancients
teach me
their handiwork
still present
for those with the faculties
to see it
shining
stronger than ever
now

Though ever appreciative
of the life nourishing
need
for darkness too
to be ever present

The spaces betwixt
or more those
that conscientiously aim
to hold space
there
anger both
those only of the sky
and their opposites
those only of nature

side taking
'twas never my preference
illusions of each
easy to shed
while also holding space
for each's necessities

YET NOT ALL BETWEENS
ARE MEANT FOR US

A you really
can't write this shit
moment
has to be witnessed
and relayed
in raw
uncensored
sensing
I wish you could see
the trilogy spread
before me
in this very perfect moment
the one wherein
this was recorded

A warm hearth
I am looking out
from beside
an Oregon coast sunset
behind me
and on one side
to the right
a sign
for storytellers
plural
an open ended

open mic
upon a piano
on gifted loan
in loving memory
of a Scottish mother
bland and earthly tones
on the surface
with pictures
as windows
of heron
of eagle
of rivers
wild and free
surrounding it
an open invitation
for any
to play music
of their own choosing
with two requests
to not place drinks
on the piano itself
and to not stand
on the bench

On the other side
to the left

symbolized
by a constructed
domestic jungle
and a heartwarming pull
for indigenous
women recentering
justice inspiring
revolutionary
social dreams
a doorway
of crystals
and rainbows galore
centered in it
with a sign
for adventurers
for an after party
music series
of select musicians
leading to
a river corridor
actively
torn up below
terribly so
to construct the look
of a healthy
modern river
amidst a muck

of slackwater's
exemplary model
with chains
chains on all pillars
and barricades
and signs a plenty
about what one
can and cannot do
and about where one
can and cannot move

Oh,
but situated
in the space between
right there in high center
like a scorching hot
midday sun
turning everything
in sight
into contrasted
shadows
and washed out
low quality light
synchronicity's laughter
a joke from Divinity
as though speaking
to me

or those that make the time
to take it all in
in presence
a sign
a representation
of Solomon's nature,
a tribute to voting,
and a crab grab
literally
written upon it
and I can't stop laughing
as a well intentioned
couple
stand centered
below it
educating a crew
of recent immigrants
on investment strategies
for how to get rich
here
most quickly
here in America
but the world really
it's all about real estate
so they say
and I can't stop laughing
that I am here

in this here and now
to observe the whole
of it
just
like
it is
before me
and yet
no two's lives
would've led them
divinely
to've seen this scene
the same
would they've

There is a sign
on the hearth though
cheaply taped up
that tonight
of all nights
'tis an early close
fireside
a private party
only
so clearly
not for me
thus subtly suggesting

that in this
circumstance
the middle ground
for just observing
has a finite
end date
for me
I wouldn't want
to get caught up
in
overstaying
my stay

So,
does one move towards
the rainbow door
as though glistening
on the surface
obscuring
its muddied promises
beyond it
wildness chained,
towards the high center
self-tagged also
Lame.
period included,
or rather towards

Celtic heart songs
beckoning
with all its promises
real or imagined
of its own
time immemorial
visions of wildness
aloft
as ushered in
upon clouds

Did I mention
I saw an eagle
fly right overhead me
just on my way
to where I sit

Is there much question
as to which
this wild heart
picked

NAMESAKE

Don't be afraid
to move in a way
so that
only the wild
can track ya

ACKNOWLEDGEMENTS

Let me begin this closing, in a rather ironic of places. I am so grateful for the dark magick workers in the world. Especially those who are lifted up to come across as guiding lights for others while invoking black magick holdings covertly. They have been instrumental teachers in leading me to see the whole of the world differently. While I disagree with the soul and web-based implications, as in web of wyrd, after all I have experienced, I would not want it any other way. Not anymore. Not at this stage. Hindsight, much easier to say.

It's so essential a part of Creation to be visible in the most subtle of nuanced ways all throughout world making. Never again will such works have pull on my heart. To be care free from that, is a freedom unlike much of anything else. Thus, I also cannot say with any clarity that the release of black magick's workings upon and through me would ever have been seen without their bondage and full ownership over it.

Having said that, I am beyond appreciative for those who have consciously or innately, instinctively or intentionally, risen above, bring awareness to, or simply sidestep black magick altogether. Those who give it little to no credence, those whose works are living examples of seemingly conscientious objections to its working in the world, and in doing so, are already living the pathway I dreamed imperative long ago. To those outcreating it, to those who will, to the starvation of such takings' ends. To you, I am forever grateful.